LIBRARY OF
AWESOME ANIMALS

FLAMINGO

By Rachel Rose

BEARPORT
PUBLISHING

Minneapolis, Minnesota

Credits

Cover and title page, © AndreAnita/iStock; 3, © yanta/iStock; 4–5, © artpritsadee/Adobe Stock; 6, © yanta/iStock; 7, © VanWyckExpress/iStock; 9, © Images01/Shutterstock; 10, © Uryadnikov Sergey/Adobe Stock; 11T, © lnichetti/Adobe Stock; 11B, © Vermeulen-Perdaen/Adobe Stock; 13, © nmessana/iStock; 14, © Gerald Corsi/iStock; 15, © zulufriend/iStock; 17, © Olga Donchuk/iStock; 18, © Roman Bjuty/iStock; 19, © Dr Ajay Kumar Singh/Adobe Stock; 21, © tane-mahuta/iStock; 22L, © Naddiya/iStock; 22R, © Esfir Dzhyshkariani/iStock; 23, © YULIIA LAKEIENKO/iStock.

Bearport Publishing Company Product Development Team

President: Jen Jenson; Director of Product Development: Spencer Brinker; Managing Editor: Allison Juda; Associate Editor: Naomi Reich; Associate Editor: Tiana Tran; Art Director: Colin O'Dea; Designer: Kayla Eggert; Product Development Assistant: Owen Hamlin

STATEMENT ON USAGE OF GENERATIVE ARTIFICIAL INTELLIGENCE

Bearport Publishing remains committed to publishing high-quality nonfiction books. Therefore, we restrict the use of generative AI to ensure accuracy of all text and visual components pertaining to a book's subject. See BearportPublishing.com for details.

Library of Congress Cataloging-in-Publication Data.

Names: Rose, Rachel, 1968- author.
Title: Flamingo / by Rachel Rose.
Description: Minneapolis, Minnesota : Bearport Publishing Company, [2025] | Series: Library of awesome animals | Includes bibliographical references and index.
Identifiers: LCCN 2023059637 (print) | LCCN 2023059638 (ebook) | ISBN 9798892320207 (library binding) | ISBN 9798892324984 (paperback) | ISBN 9798892321457 (ebook)
Subjects: LCSH: Flamingos--Juvenile literature. | Flamingos--Behavior--Juvenile literature.
Classification: LCC QL696.C56 R67 2025 (print) | LCC QL696.C56 (ebook) | DDC 598.3/5--dc23/eng/20240125
LC record available at https://lccn.loc.gov/2023059637
LC ebook record available at https://lccn.loc.gov/2023059638

For more information, write to Bearport Publishing, 5357 Penn Avenue South, Minneapolis, MN 55419.

Contents

AWESOME

Flamingos!

SPLISH, SPLASH! A group of bright pink flamingos walks gracefully through **shallow** water. With their large bodies and colorful feathers, flamingos are awesome!

THE NAME *FLAMINGO* COMES FROM THE SPANISH AND PORTUGUESE WORD MEANING FLAME-COLORED.

Pretty in Pink

There are six **species** of flamingos and all are known for their stunning appearance. These beautiful birds have bright pink, orange, or red feathers covering most of their bodies. Their long necks curve into an S-shape, and their heads have large, downward-pointing beaks. Flamingos complete their iconic look with tall, stick-like legs and webbed feet.

FLAMINGOS OFTEN STAND ON ONE LEG. THEY EVEN SLEEP THAT WAY!

Shallow Water Homes

Flamingos can be found in warm areas of the Americas, Europe, Africa, and Asia. They spend a lot of their time in shallow bodies of water, such as lakes and lagoons. Their long legs allow them to **wade** into slightly deeper water while keeping most of their feathered bodies dry.

MOST FLAMINGOS LIVE AROUND WATER THAT IS TOO SALTY FOR MANY OTHER ANIMALS TO SURVIVE.

Run, Flap, Fly!

How do such big birds fly? They begin with a running start! Flamingos use their webbed feet to run on top of the water while they flap their long wings. Once they've gained enough speed, they take off. The birds can travel as far as 370 miles (600 km) in a single flight and can reach speeds of up to 35 miles per hour (55 kph).

THE WINGSPAN OF A FLAMINGO CAN STRETCH UP TO 5 FEET (1.5 M) ACROSS.

Better Together

Flamingos are social birds. They travel and rest in large groups called flamboyances (flam-BOY-uhn-siz). Each group can have hundreds or even thousands of birds.

HONK, HONK! A flamboyance can be quite noisy! The birds **communicate** with one another by honking, grunting, and growling. Some sounds warn of danger, while others let the flock know where there is food.

THE LARGEST FLOCK OF FLAMINGOS LIVES IN AFRICA. IT IS MADE UP OF ABOUT TWO MILLION BIRDS!

Dining In

A flamingo doesn't have to go far to find food. It eats mostly shrimp and **algae** from its watery home. First, a flamingo stamps its feet to stir up the mud. Then, the bird plunges its head upside down in the water. Small comb-like parts inside its beak **filter** out water and dirt so the bird is left with just a tasty meal. *YUM!*

FLAMINGOS GET THEIR BRIGHT COLOR FROM **PIGMENTS** FOUND IN THE FOOD THEY EAT.

Danger!

While these colorful beauties have few **predators**, they sometimes need to watch out for big snakes and large cats. But sadly, the biggest danger to flamingos comes from humans.

Some people take flamingo eggs to eat or sell. Others destroy the birds' **habitats** to make space for new buildings and roads. Luckily, there are groups working to protect flamingos and their homes.

THE MAKING OF SALT ON ONE ISLAND IN THE BAHAMAS HAS CREATED MORE SHALLOW, SALTY WATER FOR FLAMINGOS TO LIVE IN.

Dance Moves

When it's time to **mate**, it's time to dance! Hundreds of flamingos get close and move together. This helps the birds find a partner. After a few weeks of dancing, the flamingos pair off and build nests. **Female** flamingos usually lay one egg at a time. Then, the parents take turns sitting on the egg to keep it warm.

FLAMINGOS USE THEIR BEAKS TO BUILD MUD NESTS THAT CAN BE UP TO 2 FT. (0.6 M) TALL.

Good Parents, Cute Babies

About 30 days later, the baby **hatches** from the egg. The proud parents feed the little gray chick something called crop milk. They make this red liquid in their throats. After a few weeks of drinking crop milk, the baby is ready to find food on its own.

It takes a few years and a lot of pigment-filled food for a young flamingo's feathers to turn beautiful shades of pink.

FLAMINGOS CAN LIVE FOR MORE THAN 40 YEARS, WHICH MAKES THEM SOME OF THE LONGEST-LIVING BIRDS.

FLAMINGOS ARE AWESOME!
LET'S LEARN EVEN MORE ABOUT THEM.

Kind of animal: Flamingos are birds. Like all birds, they are warm-blooded, are covered in feathers, and have wings.

More flamingos: The Greater Flamingo is the largest species of flamingo. It is the species with some of the brightest colors, too.

Size: Flamingos can be up to 5 ft. (1.5 m) tall. That's taller than a small car!

FLAMINGOS AROUND THE WORLD

Arctic Ocean

EUROPE

ASIA

NORTH AMERICA

Pacific Ocean

Atlantic Ocean

AFRICA

Pacific Ocean

SOUTH AMERICA

Indian Ocean

AUSTRALIA

N W E S

Southern Ocean

ANTARCTICA

WHERE FLAMINGOS LIVE

Glossary

algae tiny plantlike living things often found in lakes, ponds, and other bodies of water

communicate to share information between two or more things

female a flamingo that can lay eggs

filter to remove unwanted materials by passing them through something

habitats places in nature where plants and animals normally live

hatches breaks out of an egg

mate to come together to have young

pigments substances that give things colors

predators animals that hunt and eat other animals

shallow not deep

species groups that animals are divided into according to similar characteristics

wade to walk through shallow water or mud

Index

Read More

Lim, Angela. *Bird Behavior (Animal Behavior).* Minneapolis: Abdo Publishing, 2024.

Riggs, Kate. *Flamingos (Amazing Animals).* Mankato, MN: The Creative Company, 2023.

Learn More Online

1. Go to **www.factsurfer.com** or scan the QR code below.
2. Enter "**Flamingo**" into the search box.
3. Click on the cover of this book to see a list of websites.

About the Author

Rachel Rose writes books for kids and teaches yoga. Her favorite animal of all is her dog, Sandy.